GOD
The Final Frontier

ROBERT De LUCK

VANTAGE PRESS

New York   Washington   Atlanta   Hollywood

ORDER FROM:
Robert DeLuck
P.o. Box 460
Tijeras, N. Mexico 87059

Dedicated to:

ALL CREATION

PREFACE

GOD—THE FINAL FRONTIER will be interpreted many ways by many people, for I too have drawn conclusions.
Whatever strikes you as being truthful, realize that you're not walking to a different beat of the drum;
the drum is vibrating accordingly.

GOD

THE FINAL FRONTIER

LET THERE BE LIGHT

He said one day, "Let there be light."
    But very few can see it,
And many suffer needlessly, but don't
    know how to relieve it.
We rush along each given day, bypassing
    God's given neighbor.
Our main concern's our daily return—
    paid fruits of our everyday labor.
He told us once, "Whatever ye sow, ye shall
    also reap."
He also knows the answer lies within
    ourselves, not over the mountain steep.
We sleep at night, supposedly to rest our
    weary soul—
Don't take the time to thank the One,
    Who made us as a whole.
I tell you this, my friend, I'm neither sad
    nor sorry;
I spend my time praying for others,
    hoping to find His glory.

LIFE

If all would learn to use me wisely, the stay
could be heaven on earth.
You read of me now, but do you know of what you
read?
If not, you must use me again.
I must introduce myself once again, for most
have forgotten and abused my presence.
I do play an important part in the overall
plan—taught many right, from other than,
helped all presence rise above trial and error,
took away the negative and gave what was fair.
Upon completion of this lesson, there be ever more
to learn. Fear not though;
I be with you even when animate and inanimate
make the change,
for I am part of the All,
and All contains my part,
and my part contains also the same—
my part of the Part is called,

Life.

WHO ARE YOU AND WHERE DO YOU COME FROM?

I am like you, and I know that I'm part
  of a mass of others like me.
You see,
  I'm made of spirit like all things.
But within me, there is another force that
  gives me life.
When one is ill, I am also.
  Whatever the cause may be, I cannot
    tell.
  People call me sickness.
    Physicians call me cell.
One ill cell can cause many
  others to deteriorate.
The same also applies to the
  negative thought force in
One man.

A DESTINATION

I felt like going over there at first,
     but now I've become so involved with
the space between me and my destination,
     that it's enhanced the original
goal by revealing Beauty along the way.

Now I realize the original thought was
     beautiful before acting,
and the trip going will only make it more so.

No one knows for sure the pain
   he can endure
when pressures mount.
   So never let up; keep
your faith,
   your thoughts and deeds do
      count.

THOUGHTS DO REPAY

If I assist your gaining fame and fortune, your
name be in lights—mine be as the assistant—
will you one day be willing to take the place
of me. . .
the assistant?

If it be . . .

greatly you be rewarded upon doing so, for your
thought and deed have made you what you are,
and what you are to become.
On this path no man can justly call you liar . . .
or cheat, for
his thought cannot influence the implanted seed of
truth.

Man keeps running from the very
  things he creates . . . .
Is there ever an ending end to
  his ignorance and greed?

The more material one gains,
the more of self one loses!

So often man dreams of power . . . . . .
I wonder what his reaction
would be if he discovered the mysteries
behind the God-power that existence
            naturally
holds?

THE JOURNEY

Father!

As I journey towards truth, I find there are
many roads leading in various directions which
all seem worthy.
Which do I follow?
Do I walk one path?
Or do I walk a little on each, and boast that
          I've covered
much ground? But . . . .

I fear this direction . . . . for some speak no more
          wisely
than a lost child,
while others simply say words.
I tried everything, and did everything I
          possibly
could.
Now I'm turning my thoughts over to You.
I feel that I will be divinely guided,
and the path I'm to follow
will be lighted with Your presence.

I didn't know what it was, and yet, I wanted it.

PROSPERITY

Look at all the nice things that man
has accomplished.
Look over there!
That land harbored frogs and fish.
Now an office building occupies the land
so dozens of people can provide for their
families.
What happens when there are too many
buildings
and not enough land to grow what is
necessary
to survive?
Prosperity is good for business, but
what about
humanity?

THE VEHICLE

You call me to visualize your house . . . .
    of which house do you speak?
The house that only the eye can see?
    All the things I see in your house are
Beautiful and make the physical warm, but
    will YOU miss these possessions upon
Transition and still keep your thoughts
    at this level?
What of the other half?
    —the half you've neglected, but which now
      seeks
Guidance.
    Would it not be satisfying to depart from
      this
Level with all its beauty and still
      maintain
    a house of plenty . . . .
Knowing that all things that are . . . . .
    and were . . . .
Are still to be had?

So many are entangled in a web of
a material world that they have
forgotten what it feels like to
have a moment of peace and
serenity.

So many have so much . . . .

and yet . . . .

they really have   nothing.

NEW BUILDINGS RISING . . . .
FACTORIES BLARING . . . .
PROSPERITY SCREAMING . . . . .
THEN,
THE VOICE OF
    God.

Why should I answer to you,
when . . . .
you too . . . .
are lost?

THE CHRIST WITHIN

Everyone running,
        searching,
      hoping,
        dreaming . . .
            trying to find who they
                     are and
            what purpose they may
                     serve.

Some have asked others for guidance or a
word of comfort, but only to find that they,
too, are searching.

After

all outward seeking has left you
disillusioned and
with no answer of truth,
turn your thoughts inward.
The greatest Guide of all Guides dwells
within your
very own house.
This is the Christ within each and every
one of us.
Through Him
you shall know and have all that you seek.

As I sit here and stare at all
    creation, I can hear with my
eyes; if I were blind, I would
    see what my ears, for all things
are possible through Him.

As troubled as you may consider yourself—
Observe others.

As you listen externally . . . .
you learn the ways of the world.

When you listen internally . . . .
you learn the ways of the Kingdom.

It's a beautiful day; the sun is
shining, and all nature is
awakening from a long hard winter.
Birds sing and once again you
enjoy life with a
friend . . . .
Life itself.

FEELINGS DO FEEL

I feel the same as you do inside;
  my heart beats as yours,
My body tingles when loved,
  I roam the hills as you,
I awake in the morning as you,
  pass the time of day as you,
And my feelings hurt the same as you.

    So one day, I asked God. I said, "If I
      do all these things like he, then am
    I not part of the All also?

God spoke and said, "Why do you worry?
  Do you not act upon all things?
Do you not bring joy to all things?
  Do you not bring love to all things?
For all these things you have equally with others;
  others have all but one.
Others can only feel you, but not be you.
  For this reason I have named you,
      Feelings."

A WAY OF EXPRESSING

Why are the new ones always accepted so
graciously?
They haven't yet walked where the old have
been—
haven't dreamed what the old have accomplished—
haven't heard what the old have said—
haven't begun to feel what the old have felt.

The old were once young and vibrant, but now they
feel the law of change.
This doesn't take away their worth.
It's nature's expression of Wisdom and
          Understanding—
Ravaged faces but strong spirits.

Why contemplate illusions?
Get to the source.

What is fear?

Many journey through life fearing fear,
causing disharmony in their own lives
and in all life around them.

Therefore,

denounce fear as a reality,
for it is a contradiction to the
Divine plan of existence.

It's been said, repeatedly, that
        the wall between life and
death is a fine thin line.

    (Think about that next time
    you belittle someone.)

Relax,
Release your tensions,
Raise your faith.

The healing forces of the Universe
can then flow
                    F
                      R
                        E
                          E
                            L
                              Y

What's in a name when all things
      are the same?
He made all things related;
      mountains reaching . . .
        towards moonlight . . . shining . . .
These are but two He created.

LIFE IS LIKE FIRE . . . .

It starts with a spark and
            grows
                  and grows
                        and grows
                        and
                              GROWS.

If man cannot rise and express
his God-given Feelings,
    then
        what purpose has he in this
        life or any other Life?

CONSTRUCTIVE CRITICISM

So many people are always pouring forth
                                    suggestions
but no one really knows what they say.
Some label it Constructive Criticism.
Do this.
Do that.
People should consider that what they see may
                                    be an
illusion, which can have flaws . . .
and may therefore be in need of repair.
Comforting words are seldom meant to comfort.

So . . . .

why not push aside the illusions,
including Constructive Criticism,
and put all your faith in God?

Before
criticizing my action
or thought,
show me
your state
of
Perfection.

REFLECTIONS DO REFLECT

They say if you wish to have a fruitful life—with
all the things you desire, God will give them to
you upon asking.

Lately it seems as though I'm at a standstill . . .
for I keep striving but never attain.
Something is missing . . . .
what do I lack that others seem to have?

One concerned friend told me that upon waking I
should look at myself in the mirror and ask myself
if I were putting my best efforts forward to gain
the things that I desire.
I did this one day and discovered that the
reflection wasn't reflecting all that I thought
it should.
Maybe this is the reflection that's been
limiting me.

This must be the reflection that people see . . .
and yet . . . . . .
I've been so blind,

This is right!
That is right!
Organizers organize.
Teachers teach.
And . . . .

        There is a need for knowledge
        among the knowledgeable.

WHAT IS SOCIETY?

Society is a conglomeration of peoples who think
and feel that their way is best to express life.
The pressures of "don't do this . . . don't do that"
may be too regimented for some . . .
but . . .
what will Society say?
One man refuses to abide by the man-made rules, so
Society says he is not a fitting subject for the
Community . . .
but . . . . by the same token . . . .
the people that turned him away . . . . kill for sport
at leisure.
This man led a clean life . . .
respected mankind . . . . and loved life, but Society
didn't approve of his method.
As sure as the sun rises each morning . . .
the same men who turn their brother away will
also one day be turned away.
Upon transition . . .
they too will meet their Judge . . . and He will decree
a thing . . . and they will obey . . . and He will place
them according to their level of consciousness.

Listen, people, and listen well!
Before acting and condemning, realize that the flesh
is only temporary . . . .
but the spirit goes on and on . . .
forever.

No man is successful only
    for himself . . . .
His accomplishments are an influence
    on mankind.

No one race of people is really to
blame for a selected way of
life . . . . . .

It is the unification of thought power
that decides the fate of existing
conditions.

COLOR

Does not color vibrate like the very
   source that created it?
This is God's way of saying, "I love you."
   He gave us the various colors so
That good things and thoughts may emanate
   from them.
Be then not afraid to love all things . . .
   for all things are a vibration of God.
Be then not afraid to love all peoples . . .
   for this is also a vibration of God.
Be then not afraid to love all things
   and all peoples . . .
For all vibrations are a vibration of God,

If all men would learn to bear
their own crosses they would
discover how perfect
they were meant to be.

If more than one gather
    and some chose to do rather
while others form a dominion,
    is this group right, and
that group wrong, because both
    did voice their opinion?

It's amazing how someone loves
    you dearly
        when they know you agree with
            them . . . .
                Purely.

If I had the power to sit
         in that tower,
I'd call the world a new
         name.
I wouldn't be partial,
         prejudiced, or biased;
I'd Feel my creations the
         same.

Believe in togetherness.
To segregate
Is to separate from the All.

Man-made precepts hurl
        humiliation and jest
at the Creator when they
        preach rules and regulations
men don't adhere to themselves.

VIRTUE

If you are inclined to assist
      someone . . . . . .
Do so because you really want to . . . .
      not because it's the thing to do.

SHARING

In the process of creating a reality,
  avoid making your fellow man
      inferior.

Bring him into your thought and make him
realize that he is part of what is about
to happen.

Why can't the world work together
as one complete unit
for the perfect result?

WHAT'S IN A DOCUMENT?

The law of truth is within you;
It is made by God—
not man.

Are documents necessary to express truth and honesty?

A man spent his life in many hours
    of practice and research, but his final
reward was disaster.
    Why did he need to pursue
such intense study, if fate had already
marked him for tragedy?

Experience is the best teacher
As long as you remain alive
To appreciate the lesson.

He's out there somewhere . . .
    I know.

    No one could create anything so
        vast,
            and then,

                vanish.

To think about it
  influences you
To think about it.

Loneliness is an attitude that people
  acquire when they fail to Understand.

Facts . . . .
   figures . . . .
      assumptions . . . .
         possibilities . . . .
           and yet,

Truth existed long before all.
Unfortunately,
It is least recognized.

Although the mathematical
          valuation of
a musical quarter-note is
accepted universally, individual
concept and interpretation do create
          a different value.
In a sense, God is expressed in
          somewhat
the same way . . . .
He's a personal and individual
     expression.

A scholar counsels through acquired
knowledge from his reasoning . . . .
but a man of truth . . . .
needs no books.
His understanding is light enough
for all to see.

Whistling winds whining,
     the Magna's signing,
Who gave them their little
     old name?
We say things are equal—
     including all people.
Yet life is lived as
     a game.

Three . . . .

is such a pretty number . . . .
it designates, and illustrates, that
with a unification of two . . . .

another vibrating thing is created.

THE SOURCE

Father, I could go on and on thanking You
for all the beautiful things You have
done for me. And yet, one of the greatest
gifts You have given me is the ability to
realize Your Ever-Presence.
I need not wait for time to make its
impression upon my soul, for I know that
before time was, I was also.
I need not sit in silence, or force my
love upon the gift of woman, for
I know that within my being there is a
greater love that gives all and conquers all.
This force I know, Father,
I know, Father, as You.

'Tis easy to satisfy the carnal
through woman;

Blessed be the woman that satisfies my
soul!

It's difficult to understand people.

Their attitudes mask their
feelings.

No one knows for certain,
      what decides the final
Curtain after your programmed
      stay.
If you've lived honestly
      I feel most surely,
He'll give you another day.

WHAT IS DEATH?

Man often speaks of death and surmises
    what the outcome may be . . . but he
Never really sees it until he meets
    it face to face.

Is anything ever really . . . .
                                                    dead?

Even the voice of death . . . . .
    expresses . . . . . .
        feelings.

MORNING IT IS NOT

Tis not the morning that maketh a man;
   nor is it the four seasons.
There are no promises that morning will
ever come, or the evening with its
Heavens shining.
   Be aware of Now, and feel only Now; for Now
Is the thought that was given to use, and
   enjoy . . . . Now!

Why abuse Now?
   If it be morning Now, and your thoughts are
For the evening . . . you are then abusing the
   gift of Now.
Is not thought a product of Now?
   So why abuse Now? It irritates the soul.

   This act will only make you unhappy . . . .
Now.

GROWING

Why dwell on your past when there is so
    much waiting for you in the future?
Try to recognize that the energy spent
    thinking of past events can be
       utilized for creating new
          thoughts for the future.
            And when the time
                is right . . . .
living the now, will only be possible
    through shedding of the past.

As man grows old . . . .
    his expressing of fear, pain, and suffering,
    reveals
    that he knows the true meaning of experience.

For a man to grow, he must push away the
topsoil and experience all the natural
functions of life . . . .
including the not-so-pleasant.

—A TREE SPEAKS—

A tree is looked upon as a tree by most, but why
        can't I be loved as man loves woman?
Am I not equal in value in God's eye?
Am I to be used only as a tree?

If this be true, then woman is equal to me, for does
not man use woman and only as so?

I go through trials and errors that man creates, and
yet I'm only a tree.
Are not I part of God's plan also?

I do give of myself—and even more, and yet I'm still
looked upon only as a tree.
If I were a leader of men, I could not do to man
what man does to me.

TIME

Time exists and lives as you.
It has its moments of depression and desires
which are often heard by those who listen.
And those who listen
exist with time.

Time reveals much wisdom with age.
Others express time as it is known
through age.

Youth accomplishes many wonders with time, as
time does equally so
with youth.

You like to use time as seems fit.
So . . . .
time gives you the time to do so.

It takes time to learn of something that
exists with our every move.
So take your time . . . .
For time will give you the time to do so.

HOW TO GIVE

I can't do everything myself.
Someone must assist me.
If I thirst, hopefully someone will
give me water.
But I cannot dispute the manner in which
he gives,
for I am in dire need.

If a tree be dry through drought, and a
              raging flood
comes to tear it from its very roots,
what good shall this water be?

Therefore . . . . .
upon giving . . . .
give with good intent . . . . .
or the giving may be useless.

WHAT CAN I GIVE?

I did ask and I did receive, but now I know not
    what to give.

What to give troubles my mind, for I
    want everything I have.
Besides . . .
What could anyone want from me?
Everything that I have came from someone else; so
    what can I possibly give to anyone?

Can it be material gain?

What can it be?
        I know what it is!

I'm to give the same feeling to everyone that I
    received when I received all that I asked for.

AN ASKING

Father!
As I lay my weary body to rest after another
given day, my spirit still remains high
and awake.
It recognizes what You do for me when I ask
for Your guidance.
My spirit rejoices when I ask not for riches and
fame, for it knows that they are borrowed for a
spell.
The strength that I ask to carry me through my
everyday life is what my spirit enjoys.
It also knows that collecting the material
only burdens the spirit.
Opening myself and receiving this constant flow of
energy You offer, I will recharge my vehicle,
and all dreams . . . .
will become a reality.

The signs says, "Speed limit 50 miles an hour,"
    which is good. But many men fall
short of their goals because
    they settle for . . . .
                                    limits.

DO I NEED INSURANCE?

Today a man gave of himself in an effort to design
insurance in my life.
It was good, but the plan could only pay
dividends to the physical without consideration
for the spirit.
If I were to accept his plan, then all I believe
would be a form of hypocrisy, for my true faith
and trust are in God.
For this reason I cannot accept his plan, for I
know that God has already prepared a divine plan
for me and my every need . . . .

both physical . . .
and spiritual.

A RETURN TICKET

I've finally returned and this time it will
be different for me.

I'll do all the things I missed . . . .
see all there is to see . . .
have all there is to be had . . . .

My last stay was rather difficult, but during
              that
time a spark of wisdom was given to me to
              help me
realize what great wonders are at my disposal
              this time.
Now I have a Pre-paid Eternal Realization
              Ticket. All I
have to do is learn to sit back and develop
              myself
as part of the ride.

SETTING THE PACE

During this life, I was exposed to so many
uncomfortable conditions and circumstances
that I almost lost faith.
Suddenly I regained my energy, and realized that
Faith was responsible for carrying me through, when
hope was gone.
I simply turned my thoughts inward to establish
and feel the presence of God running through my
every cell—and with this—
my faith was restored and vibrant with life.
I now have the strength to accept the bad as
good, and overcome all obstacles with ease.
I hope that my faith in faith will be an example
for one of the many . . . for if one of the many sees
the good . . . .
then he too . . . .
shall be an example.

UNDERSTANDING

Understand what, Father?

I need not spend time gaining knowledge that
only feeds my physical,
casting my spirit aside to lie withered and
                              wasted.

Tis the spirit that motivates the physical . . .
Is it not?

Then why should I neglect the source from which
the physical receives its strength?

I understand that my stay here is for a purpose,
and part of Your divine plan for me,
but why didn't You give me the knowledge to
understand Your works?

Oh!
Now I understand.

THE ALL OF EVERYTHING

What I have to say cannot be measured in writing,
for all things have existed before time was.
Hear Me now!
With patience and listening, you shall gain all
there is to know of what you seek.
You need not wait for one particular teacher, for
you are much in tune with All. And All sees that
you are. And with this, you will give many an
understanding.
You have been chosen to do much for all and All
knows this.

I WONDER

A bird sang today, but of what
I know not, for I know not
yet of my own song.
Of my song I know the bird
sings, for I can hear, but I know
not if he hears my song. The
bird sings; my mind thinks.
I wonder if this bird and I can be
related?

I am a student of truth and realize
    that Your Ever-Presence will
assist me in overcoming all obstacles
    that fall on my path.
Each day I strive to
    know what
Some only know as a word . . . .
    and yet,
I know not what to say.

NEGLIGENCE

Dear Father,
    Please forgive me for not communicating
with You the past few days. I've been rather
busy with my daily life and didn't realize that
I was neglecting You so. Once I stopped to think
of You, but then I was overcome with my everyday
chores and thought I'd get back to You later.
Well, it so happened that I didn't, and now I'm
asking for Your forgiveness.
How foolish of me to neglect the very Source
that supplies my everyday needs!

I want to do what I have to do in
   my lifetime, but I cannot rest.
I see there is a need for guidance
   among God's children.

I
  wonder
    what the world would be like if
      everyone
        felt
          the way I
            do?

A HUMBLE ASKING

Master,

I'm doing the best I can, applying my
                studies
and meditations,
please be patient with me.
At this time I can only thank You
                for the things You are
manifesting for me, yet I'm always
                aware of
Your presence.

What You are doing for me now will
benefit mankind throughout ages,
for I know that You have chosen me
                to express
Your great teachings.
How I am to reveal these teachings I
                do not yet know.
but I can feel that You will guide me
                when
the time is right.
When I need guidance I know that You
                will be
there to assist me in my endeavors,
                and with
Your assistance, I'll help others to
                grow, and
light a path on their journey to truth.

I am to serve as a wayshower for those
                who are
asking. And when the time is right . . . .
I too will be a perfect Master.

Learning to know God
is an eternal
quest.